This Is Hard

This Is Hard

What I Say When Loved Ones Die

Jon Swanson

Copyright © 2021 by Jon C. Swanson

All rights reserved. This book or any portion thereof
may not be reproduced or used in any manner whatsoever
without the express written permission of the author
except for the use of brief quotations in a book review.

SocialMediaChaplain.com

Author photo by Megin Hatch, meghatchphotography.com

This is number six in the series, Resources on Faith, Sickness, Grief and Doubt.

This is a work of nonfiction. Identifying characteristics have been changed to protect the privacy of individuals described.

Dedication

*These words are dedicated to you and to the
memory of the one you are grieving.*

Contents

A word from Jon   1

10 THINGS I OFTEN SAY

This is hard.   5

Of course it's hard to think.   7

People say really stupid things to hurting   9
people. They usually don't mean it.

A minute at a time may be all you can do.   11

You don't have to know every answer right   12
now.

You don't need to be strong for anyone.   14

We can feel happy for our loved one AND   16
sad for ourselves.

You get to be the center of your universe at   18
the moment.

This is not your fault.	*20*
God's not mad at you, even if you are mad at God.	*22*
You don't have to move on.	*24*
When will the stages come? Why do I feel waves of sadness?	*26*
Remember the best time, not the last time.	*28*
I thought parents were supposed to go first.	*30*
Not everyone who dies is a nice person.	*32*

JOURNAL

What's the last best memory you have?	*37*
What has surprised you the most about this time of grief?	*38*
What do you want to say to the person you are grieving?	*39*
What are the words and acts from people that helped the most?	*40*
What do you want to remember a year from now?	*41*
What do you want to never forget?	*42*
What will you never say to someone going through this?	*43*

What are the hopes and dreams that you want to keep going? *44*

What are the hopes and dreams that you are releasing? *45*

RESOURCES

Resources on Grief *49*

A word from Jon

Dear friend–

I wish I could sit with you.

No one has ever had this moment after this death of this person. And no one will again.

+++

Each time I talk with someone following the death of a loved one, I listen to their pain, I listen to their silence, I listen. And then eventually, gradually, I offer some thoughts that respond to their loss in this moment.

I'm a hospital chaplain. I've had a few hundred opportunities to listen and think and respond to parents and children and partners and siblings and friends. I've also walked through loss as a son, a father, a grandfather, a brother-in-law, a friend. I've been on your side of the bed in these moments for my parents and our daughter.

I've found that some thoughts seem to be helpful for more than one person. And so I've gathered some of those here. Read them all at once or as you need them.

Although I know not everyone is a journaling person, I've given you some space to write some of your own words, as you walk through the next days and decades.

This isn't a book to read through. I wouldn't say all of these things all at once. It's more like a conversation where you can bring a question, read and set aside and read and toss across the room and read and write in and reread.

Though this is written by a hospital chaplain, I'm not going to preach. Instead, as we go forward, I'm praying for your peace.

And don't forget to eat something. I know that doesn't sound spiritual. But you will forget to eat. And you need to eat.

10 Things I Often Say

Actually, there are more than ten things. I just wanted you to get your attention with the title, and then tell you that there is a human writing these words, someone who knows that there aren't formulas or lists or recipes for this moment.

I don't expect you to read these words all at once. That's why the chapter titles are responses to questions people ask and feelings people have.

You can choose which ones you need right now. And come back for others later.

This is hard.

I used to say, "I'm sorry for your loss." Most people are polite when they hear it. It's better, I suppose, than never saying anything. Then one friend said, "I hate that phrase."

Here's what's true: this moment is hard. You know that. And more than a vague apology for something that no one could control, you may need someone to acknowledge that this is hard.

Breathing is hard. Thinking is hard. Imagining the next few years is hard. Remembering anything is hard. Being polite is hard. Feeling numb is hard.

You can fill in some of your own hard things.

And now isn't the moment for saying. "But other people have it worse." Other people have hard things, too. And we can acknowledge that. But their hard moments don't suddenly make this moment easy for you.

Try something.

Say "THIS is hard."

Say "This IS hard."

Say "This is HARD."

And as you say it, know that I agree with you. This is hard.

Of course it's hard to think.

"I don't know why I can't remember that." I hear it all the time.

People forget how to write. People forget the names of places they have seen a hundred times.

And then people say, "I'm sorry. I can't think of that name. I can't remember my address. Why can't I think of that name?"

They, or maybe you, feel like it must be your fault that you can't remember.

I ask them not to apologize.

They, or maybe you, just had a massive disruption of everything. You are wondering about what will happen next. You are wondering what you could have done differently. You are thinking about what people will say, what people will expect from you. And, at the same time you have all these details, you are realizing that you will never have another conversation with this person.

Of course you can't think the way you wish you could. Your mind is preoccupied by questions. Your body has just had a shock.

What can you do to help yourself?

You can ask people to repeat questions. You can ask other people to answer on your behalf. You can ask for a few minutes to think or to rest. You can eat something (even if you don't feel like it).

Nothing's wrong with your thinking. Everything is wrong with your heart.

People say really stupid things to hurting people. They usually don't mean it.

The mom and dad were sitting by the bed. Their toddler was close to death. Within an hour or two, the child would be gone.

I was talking them through what was going to happen next. I said, "People are going to say things without thinking."

There are so many things people say. In one of our oldest stories of comfort that failed, Job lost his kids, his belongings, and his health. And then Job's three friends rubbed pain into his wounded heart with words of blame.

The mom nodded. She understood. And she said, "But they mean well."

She's right, of course, but she was more gracious than I would be.

What can you do?

You can smile and nod. You can avoid those people (at least for now). You can enlist a friend to be with you and protect you. You can excuse yourself to go to the restroom. You can respond with, "I know you mean well, but that's not how I feel at the moment."

You can find the people who give you life.

A minute at a time may be all you can do.

Sometimes people say, "I'm taking it a day at a time." I suggest that they take it a breath at a time, a minute at a time. In the course of a day, too many feelings come, too much uncertainty. A day, a night, a week, can feel immense, impossible.

So make it through the next minute and count it as enough of an achievement for that minute. Finding the tissue box is enough. Going to the bathroom, eating a bite of toast, looking out the window. All these are ways to take it a minute at a time.

In time, you may move to five minutes at a time. But that can wait.

Take the next breath.

You don't have to know every answer right now.

"I've never done this before. I don't know what to do."

No one is an expert on the death of their loved one, not even the people who are experienced with death.

In those moments, there are answers that we deeply want. "Why did this happen?"

I'm not comfortable answering those questions, at least not in the first days and decades after a death. Understanding the meaning of a death and of a life takes time.

However, there are other answers that we deeply want. "How do I plan a funeral?" "What happens to my mom now that dad's not here?" "What do we do with all this stuff?"

My best advice is to suggest that you find the people who have done this before. For example, funeral homes have helped people plan funerals. There are some that are mean or incompetent. Most of the ones I know are helpful and compassionate. Ask the people that you trust who they trust. (And get prices at parting.com).

For dealing with stuff, for dealing with grief, for dealing with relationships, there are cleaners and counselors and pastors and other people with experience in being helpful.

And then there is this: *You can call a time-out.* Like in a basketball game or a football game, you can say, "I can't answer that this minute, I need to catch my breath."

You don't need to be strong for anyone.

I know. You may argue with me. "I need to be strong for my kids." "I need to be strong for my mom."

If being strong means arranging for meals for your kids or making sure your mom is safe, that's fine.

If being strong means not crying in front of your kids or your mom, or not acknowledging their grief and yours, we need to chat a bit.

For my dad's generation, being strong meant "not crying". Which meant that we learned that even if your heart was breaking because a parent was dying, you shouldn't cry.

I would love to have future generations know that feelings are great, that tears are a perfect response to deep loss, that Jesus was willing to listen and weep and talk with his grieving friends.

You can be as strong or as weak as you need to be, but you don't have to do it for anyone else.

We can feel happy for our loved one AND sad for ourselves.

Often, someone says, "We should be happy for Dad. He's not suffering anymore." I look at them and carefully say, "He's not suffering, but he's not here. And you still are."

It's possible for our loved one to be doing great and for us to be hurting like hell. I use that word carefully. I'm thinking about separation. We are not able to touch them, not able to talk to them and hear a response, not able to look into their eyes and to hear their laugh (or their sarcasm).

It's the perfect example of mixed emotions. And it's completely acceptable.

You aren't lacking faith.

When Jesus wept at the grave of his friend Lazarus, he knew the short-term story and the long-term story. But he still expressed sadness.

If he could, you can.

You get to be the center of your universe at the moment.

The world is going on right now. Other people are laughing, shopping, watching TV. I'm sorry. Because in your universe right now, everything is falling apart. Everything is stopping. As much as we'd like it, we can't make everyone else stop.

But *you* can stop.

You can accept support and sympathy.

You can hurt and cry and not cry and laugh.

If someone says, "Let me know if I can do anything," you can say, "Let me cry for a bit" or "Bring me coffee" or "Listen to me tell a story about my dad" or "Please ask me in an hour." You can even say, "Could you ask those people to come back later?"

You can, for right now, resist worrying about everyone else.

You can hurt.

This is not your fault.

This death is not your fault.

It's not something God is doing to get your attention.

This isn't because you forgot to say something.

You may be thinking, "If only I could tell them one more time to take care of their health."

You may be thinking, "If only I had been listening more closely when they were talking about their struggles."

You may be thinking, "If only I had spent more time."

An ancient writer reflecting on life and death tells us that all of our days are numbered before one of them comes to be. Your grief is big enough without adding the burden of self-blame.

And be very careful about listening to the blame that others may try to assign you. Often, we lash out at others because of pain we're feeling ourselves.

Now, I'll be honest. You may have regrets about things you said or didn't, ways that you spent time. But those regrets are different than blame. We can apologize for things we regret. But for now, hear this: *"This is not your fault."*

God's not mad at you, even if you are mad at God.

"I do not understand." That's what I said to God before the graveside service for our five-week old daughter.

I wasn't mad, exactly, but I did not understand, and I wanted to be honest with God about it.

I have talked to people who are angry. Sometimes they express that anger toward people. "If only they would have listened to me when I told them to get to the doctor," they say. Some of those people are a little afraid to be angry at God, so they blame others.

But here's my picture for them.

Imagine standing with someone who had the power to save the one you loved. You start yelling at them.

"If you would have been here, my brother wouldn't have died." You start pounding on their chest with your fists. And as you do, you start to weep. And they wrap their arms around you and begin to weep, too.

That is what Martha said to Jesus. And Mary, too. Mary fell at Jesus's feet. And Jesus wept with her.

That's why I'm pretty sure that God's not mad at you in these moments of grief, even if you are mad at God.

We are talking to someone who understands how hard being human is.

You don't have to move on.

Some people will tell you that it's time to move on.

What they mean is that your tears and conversation about your grief are making them feel uncomfortable. What they mean is that they are thinking about other things and you should be, too. What they mean is that they don't know how your grief feels.

We move on after a bad decision. We move on after a broken bone heals. We move on after something ends. Except for a life. Part of who we are is because of them. And that's not something you move on from. Because we don't move on from ourselves.

Recently, I walked down the hall with a family member. "You don't have to move on," I said. She agreed.

"Instead," I said, "we go on."

When a family member or friend dies, we go on. Taking one step and then another. But we don't move on.

As Nora McInerny says, "The truth is that the things that shape us—the good and the bad—stay with us. We're RESHAPED. We are different."[1]

As we go on, as we move forward, we will remember what they thought about things, we will respond to what they would have done, we will carry them with us.

---

1. https://goop.com/wellness/spirituality/the-hot-young-widows-club/. The language of moving forward rather than moving on is from Nora.

When will the stages come? Why do I feel waves of sadness?

We've heard about them: denial, anger, bargaining, acceptance. We want a schedule for them. There is no schedule.

And so we wonder, "What if I miss a stage? What if I get stuck? I want to get it right."

Or maybe we are doing fine, maintaining our composure, and then suddenly there is a wave of sadness. Or we're crying and suddenly we start laughing. "What's wrong with me?" we ask.

Nothing is wrong with you. And you probably won't get stuck.

Grief is a response to loss, and you are sorting through all kinds of loss.

You can read more about the stages of grief. You can be aware that the waves are going to come.

But there's nothing "wrong" with you.

Remember the best time, not the last time.

I was talking to somebody recently who had lost a loved one. In the course of our conversation, they were talking about their last conversation with the person who had died. It wasn't necessarily a bad one but it wasn't a magnificent one, either. She said "If I had known it was our last time talking, I would have done something more significant. I would have said 'I love you', or something like that."

As we were talking I said, "Maybe the better thing to do is not to remember the last conversation with your loved one. Why don't you remember the best conversation that you had with your loved one."

Even as it came out of my mouth I thought, "That's a really good idea."

Often, as we remember those last conversations, we remember the question we didn't answer, the frustration we felt, the ordinariness. We are saddened by their confusion from medication or the dementia. We lament the fact that we didn't have a last conversation.

What we'd love to remember is the best conversation.

That moment when a parent told us that they loved us, a moment when we had a restoration of relationship, a moment with some clarity of mind where both of you were able to say, "This is what really matters to me. You really matter to me,"

Instead of worrying about that last conversation, start telling yourself and others about the best conversation that you had with that person. And by telling the story, you will make that be the thing you remember.

I thought parents were supposed to go first.

If you are reading these words, I'm sorry.

It means that your child has died. And whether they were stillborn or sixty, we never plan to bury our children.

Your grief has been shared by people for generations, and yet it is your grief in this moment.

Though he was the king, David wept and fasted as his child was dying. Mary the mother of Jesus stood at the cross, watching her son die.

As I look for words for you and for me in this moment, "disordered" is a good way to describe what is happening. The death of a child is out of the normal order of death. And it disorders our lives.

We had dreams and plans, we had stories that were going to be told around this child as they grew up. And the dreams and the plans and the stories are suddenly changing, too.

There isn't anything that can fix this moment.

There is just this thought, which may or may not be helpful. God knows what it's like to lose a child. And so, when we talk to God, or cry out, or holler, we are talking to (or talking at) a person who has an understanding.

Not everyone who dies is a nice person.

I once spoke at a funeral and was told afterward, "If you had praised him, I would have walked out. He abandoned us." I knew that. And my words reflected the pain I knew people had felt.

You can have conflicting feelings. You may not feel the sadness about this person that everyone is talking about. Not everyone who dies is a nice person.

We each have a different relationship with the person who died. So you can have a different response to their death.

- Sometimes we're more relieved than we are sad, because we don't have to deal with the problems any more.

- Sometimes the sadness we feel is about what everyone else got and we didn't.
- Sometimes we are frustrated because the person never apologized, never recognized the pain they caused.
- Sometimes things are just complicated.

People will tell us that they are sorry for our loss. We don't have to fill them in about how awful the person was to us. We can simply thank them for their concern for us.

And, I'm sorry. Not necessarily for the loss. But for the pain that you have had.

Journal

Sometimes it helps to write things down. It helps us remember what we might otherwise forget. It helps us to think through what we may not understand. It helps us find the words that our voices can't always find.

On the following pages are some prompts to help you write. You can write in this book, or you can write in another journal, or on a blog, or on Facebook, or on scraps of paper you will throw away.

There's not a right way to write. There is simply your way. And that will be the best way.

What's the last best memory you have?

_____
_____
_____
_____
_____
_____
_____
_____
_____

What has surprised you the most about this time of grief?

What do you want to say to the person you are grieving?

_____

_____

_____

_____

_____

_____

_____

_____

_____

What are the words and acts from people that helped the most?

_____
_____
_____
_____
_____
_____
_____
_____
_____

What do you want to remember a year from now?

_____
_____
_____
_____
_____
_____
_____
_____
_____
_____

What do you want to never forget?

What will you never say to someone going through this?

_____
_____
_____
_____
_____
_____
_____
_____
_____
_____

What are the hopes and dreams
that you want to keep going?

_____
_____
_____
_____
_____
_____
_____
_____
_____
_____

What are the hopes and dreams
that you are releasing?

_____

_____

_____

_____

_____

_____

_____

_____

Resources

Resources on Grief

Sometimes, the best help we can find is in resources we can browse at our own pace.

This is not an exhaustive list. Instead, it represents the kind of resources that are available. For an updated list, visit socialmediachaplain.com/thisishard.

Support for kids
Children often need help making sense of death. Organizations like Erin's House for Grieving Children in Fort Wayne, Indiana, and Ele's Place in Michigan provide places and programs for children in their communities. They also have online resources that can be used by anyone.

Stillbirth and miscarriage
Kristen and Patrick Riecke. *No Matter How Small:*

Understanding Miscarriage and Stillbirth. (Fort Wayne, Emerald Hope Publishing House, 2020).

Kristen and Patrick draw on their own experience and their work with parents to offer support and explanation and encouragement.

How to talk to other people about grief and finding meaning

Patrick Riecke, *How to Talk With Sick, Dying, and Grieving People: When There Are No Magic Words to Say.* (Fort Wayne, Emerald Hope Publishing House, 2018).

Patrick Riecke, *How to Find Meaning in Your Life Before it Ends.* (Fort Wayne, Emerald Hope Publishing House, 2019).

How to plan a service

Jon Swanson, *Giving a Life Meaning: How to Lead Funerals, Memorial Services, and Celebrations of Life.* (Fort Wayne, Emerald Hope Publishing House, 2020).

Learning from nature

Jason Kissel, *How Trees Deal With Loss.* Fort Wayne. 2017.

This short, illustrated book from a tree guy shows us how trees deal with the loss of another tree, and can help us understand our own loss.

Personal stories

Listening and watching people talk about their own journey and those of others can be incredibly helpful.

Podcast: "Surprised by Grief" with Clarissa Moll and Daniel Harrell. This podcast is from a Christian perspective. Each of the hosts lost a spouse in 2019. Clarissa's husband, Rob, died in a climbing accident. Daniel's wife died with pancreatic cancer. But these two had already thought about life and death more than most people. Rob wrote a book, *The Art of Dying*, several years before his death, and Daniel was working as a pastor. They talk about their own experiences and the work they are doing with others, and invite us into the conversation. The content is often hard, but listening to them interact is remarkably helpful.

Video: Nora McIerney, We don't "move on" from grief. We move forward with it, TED, 4/9/2019. In a few weeks, Nora McIerney lost her dad, her husband, and her unborn child. She writes and podcasts about grief, loss, and living. This video is key to understanding the idea of moving forward.

Book: C.S. Lewis, *A Grief Observed.* HarperOne, 2009. With a foreword by Madeleine L'Engle. C.S. Lewis is know for writing about faith and about Narnia. This is like reading a journal in the days after his wife's death. It captures the waves of grief. The foreword by Madeleine, also a writer, talks about the loss of her husband, and illustrates that each loss is different.

Jesus and grief
The story of Lazarus's death and the grief of his sisters, mentioned in this book, gives a glimpse of how Jesus was with people in grief. The story is in John 11.

More from Dr. Jon Swanson
You can find more resources from Jon and contact information for him at SocialMediaChaplain.com.